POEMS IN MY DRAFT PAD

A STORY OF LIFE, CONSISTING OF LIVES

SARANYA NARAYANA MOORTHY

Made with ♥ on the Notion Press Platform
www.notionpress.com

To every Episode of my daily life,

To every person, I ever met,

To every Netflix Episode, I watched,

In every Fiction, I ever read,

To every creator, I follow on Instagram & LinkedIn..

Reading all the stories, every person, every emotion has given me a new perspective I wouldn't have acquired if I was always drowned in my own world. So Thanks for making my world bigger and making my perspective wider.

Special Dedication: To the Butterflies of my Soul & the Sky.

Contents

Contents

Preface

Hello Amazing Human! I have no idea why you are here, but I am glad you are here. You probably might know who I am or you might want to discover who I was and who i wanted to be. But let me tell you this - In this process you will not just discover me, but you will also discover who you wanted to be, or atleast gain a perspective of what life looks like for another person probably with a story and heart full of life.

I might not be the best person who has lived so far, but to me - I have lived the best life ever and I wouldn't want it any other way. So now - let me take you through a few episodes of what I call, my 'realisations of life' and in some places, just a 'nourishing capture of MY BEST MOMENTS' filled with Love, Emotions and Free Will in every letter of the Poem.

So that being said, Let me take you through every poem that made its way from my curious mind to the Draft Pad and actually approved by the Star.

Prologue

When I thought Life was a Mess - the Sky made me laugh hard.

When I thought Life was a Bliss - Sky taught me to look at the rocks I crossed on my way there

Almost with every moving second, I was in either of the two edges. Either the one where I feel the Most Blessed or the one where I felt if I was ever destined to meet the Freedom I yearned to be in. But almost in both of these split worlds - I had this one thought, "I am at a better place than where I was yesterday, and Tomorrow I will most certainly in a better place than where I am today". And that is my mantra for going forward.

Have you heard of Immovable assets? The ones where you probably have all the assets in your name, but just can't utilise it? Sometimes life can be like that. And even worse, sometimes it would feel like you wouldn't even want to think of how it would be if it weren't movable at all. But as I say through every upcoming poem that you are going to read, '**Factually, there is certainly a light at the end of the Tunnel. But to reach the tunnel, you must be daring to travel until the end. Just becasue you don't see it - it doesn't mean it isn't there.**'

I believe, this book or any one of the poem, would help you navigate through the tunnel - until you reach the end of it. Even if one sentence did, I am contented of my purpose to have written this book.

Let's travel together.

1. Sensuality - The 20 Poems of Quarter Life Crisis

It's not the senses. It's the sensuality. That makes a human a HUMAN.

Senses keep you Sane. Sensuality reckons insanity.

Be insane. Be alive.
The following are the 20 poems I would want you to read. Some about Cries, some about Laughter. Some about Hate, some about Love. Some about Loyalty, Some about Betrayal. But each of them - holding a piece.
A piece of the story we call Life.
ps: They are in no particular order. Feel Free to Flip/Scroll through any page and give it a read.

The First Spark

The first spark that I felt did not have a name. It was just comfortable.

It was beyond ordinary. I wanted it. I needed it. Every damn day.

I first discovered love in *Vinnai thaandi varuvaya.* I was 13 by then.

Crazy, I felt it a year before I discovered what it was.

Many people are in relationships. But not many experience Love. The butterflies. The feeling of seeing a thousand stars in the sky and yet - admiring that one star as if it's just yours.

Just a difference - the one you feel this with really is yours.

Life - a Poem

People say, "Life is Prose".

It's Dull and Boring. Definetly not as you see in Fiction or Movies.

Yes, it's the same people who never took the time to turn
'**Moments into Poetry.**'

Just like how, a Boquet can either be in a Proposal or a Cremation
- Life too can either be a Valley of Hope or a Deseart of
Desperation.

Question is: "How do you Make it?"

.

.

adopted from an Instagram story

Don't trust it when people say your life can't be one of those
"Happily Ever After" movies.

It can if you direct yours that way.

But generally, people are too pessimistic to give you the hope.

We often hear people saying, "Don't think of flying before you start walking"

It's okay to be precautious. But, how would you feel when people say this while you are happily visualising your dreams?

Anyone would feel discouraged. And when repeated many times, Hopeless.

But

You. Yes you. Don't need to be Hopeless.

Because today, you are seeing this as a sign to start making your life, a poetry.

Like those Happily Ever after Movies.

You - write - your - OWN - Poem ❤?

Start writing, right from today!

Life is 10% what happens to us, 40% how we take it & 50% how we think about it.

Change your perspective & Change your life.

The Sun's Virginity

"Bold, Dominant, suppressing anything else in the sky."

"Bright, Providing for Everyone, On Top of the World"

"THE SUN IS A STAR"

POV: The Sun

"I'm Happy, feeling Superior, King of the World; if not for me - the World would sink in Darkness."

"Proud, Brave, Powerful, Embracing the Chest, Bright, Above everyone & everything."

As I go home.. wait! Do I ever go home? Or, Do I ever have a Home? Because I feel, 24 hours a day, I'm at a place where someone expects me to "PROVIDE" for them. All I feel is taking shifts between the Southwest & Northeast Hemisphere may be one of which you call a Home.

At times, when I get tired, I hide behind the clouds. Sometimes people are relieved that I'm hiding & sometimes, they yell.

Sometimes they look upto me, sometimes I only hear, "The Fucking Sun!! To Hell with it".

Sometimes I'm worshipped, to an extent I never even expected it to be, and start feeling uncomfortable and sometimes cursed. But many times, I hear people speaking amongst themselves,

"Be Like the Sun. Come up & Kill people with your Heat (Kindness). Shine so bright that the rest of the world is afraid to look you straight in the eye."

I just laughed hearing this! Cuz, does anyone know how I feel?

Do you know how I feel?

I WANNA SCREAM!!!!

CRY LOUDER THAN THE WORLD'S WORST THUNDER BAWL; RUN AWAY FROM ALL OF THESE.

FYI, I do try running away. Every 12 hours, hoping to find Solace. But no matter where I go, it's the Same disappointments, same story of BEING THE SUN & you know what? I'm tired!

I tried of standing Tall & bright, tired of everything & Everyone around me.

In my lucky days, I get the company of Clouds. And every time I have them, I hide behind them. Choosing Solace, Choose a minute of peace and solitude. And sometimes, I cry out aloud. Throwing tantrums, worse than the Thunder & Lightening.

How long will I be able to hold?
Honestly, I don't know!

I was relieved when the Chinese created an artificial Sun; it was like, finally, Can I rest...? Move away from yáll...? Lead my Own Life...?

It turns out I couldn't!

"People look at me and say to themselves- I should be like the Sun. Dominant and Powerful - But in a way, no one can even touch Me! That's how high my Morality and chaste should be!"

To all of you, I just have one Question. Despite all my characteristics, you USE me every day. From Solar to Light, Heat to Warmth, Astrology to Astronomy.

So even after so many forms of Usage, Am I still a Virgin?

Dedicated to every Man who is a Father, Son, Brother, Husband, Boyfriend, or just a Man.

Life needn't be fancy; having a Tough Life for greater glory is okay. You needn't be tough all the time. Its okay to not be Okay.

Question: Do the Men in your Life feel like the Sun? If yes, Ladies - You have Failed!

The Moon's Search for Meaning

"Beautiful, Cool, Adoring, Humble, Shy, Modern yet Conservative, Takes care of the Family of Stars."

"The Bright Light of the night sky, the answer to all the darkness, Responsible for Providing Light."

POV: The Moon

Every day of my life - I have waited. Sometimes in, I hope for a better future, and sometimes, by losing myself in the depressiveness of my current life progression. Whenever I go down or be in the dark, I hear people say, "This is the dying phase." Do not start anything new.

I am blamed for their low emotions, their failures, and the way things work out.

Apparently, according to them: It's me who pulls down the Vibe of the house.

Sad. isn't it?

I do try my best.

To Bloom, to Grow. But as I reach a certain level of happiness, I come down. Something brings me down. I try to be my best, and once I am full - people bring up my deformities; they say I am IMPURE for my imperfections.

"The Full Moon - How bright it is. The Shine is Marvelous. But How pretty it would be if she doesn't have the spots she has now."

See, it's funny! With so much power within me, all they see is my deformities.
Like, should I be perfect? Are they? Should I not have my OWN share of originality?

And thus, I start spiraling down. Once again. Deep into my own depth of insecurities.

I sometimes even disappear and come back from my 'Ghosting from depression state.' and now - for a while, I am appreciated.

And then I hear this: "The Moon doesn't have a light of its own. It's the light from the Sun that it reflects."

I wonder, "Am I worthless if not for the Sun? Do you realize who put me in this position to be dependent? To expect the Sun to light Up? Do you think I am here by choice?"

No! you wouldn't realize! You would only Blame or Judge. Cus its easier, right? and I know you'll Never Realise - Perhaps its a curse, a Generational Curse! - You are all just brought up that way!

But trust me, One day - I will stand Up! and that day, you will remember:

"I DID IT ALL BY MYSELF!"

& If not for the moon - the Sun's Brightness wouldn't keep the family of stars together!

Dedicated: To Every Woman who strives hard for the family and is never recognized.

Every Housewife & Every Woman whose thoughts, were shadowed!

The Prince

Me to Me: *Why do I love him??*

Is it the eyes? The lip? The face?

Uhm,

Nope!

Is it his actions?

Uhm, not so sure.

Is it his personality/behavior?

Ugh ugh ugh, i don't know.

Is it the way he does things?

Could be!

Is it his bright and adventurous future plans?

Uhm, that's a good bonus

Oh okay! So then, if not any of it - WHAT IS IT?

Ever heard of a Magic a Soul has? A magic a MAN can have just by existing?

Ever felt the smell, the smile, the eyes, the voice was sooo intoxicating that you memorized every word he ever spoke?

Ever realized how special a person can be just by living every moment?

That's him for me.

The man whom I started loving from the soul and not from the eyes or heart.

Pick out my heart and even if it stops the next time the soul has a form it will still go searching for the prince.

Nude

Seductive Shadows or seductive poses have a evoking dominance in them that isn't just a serving for male attention but rather an expression of Female Strength & Fierce emotions.

When Navarasa expresses emotions in a conservative & traditional style as how Womanhood had portrayed it to be

Naked Paintings or seductive images represent strength that comes from the liberative free spirit.

Making the world strike-through, dominating yet controlling pride. This is the part where you look as if you are being controlled while intoxicating the Master to trigger forms of control.

Isn't it an Illusion? While it looks as if she's controlled, the truth is she Controls.

It's not the showcasing of the body that evokes these emotions but the courage to stay without an external cover. Or, in other words, the freedom to expose your true self without a hood put on top. To explore the deepest sensuality that exists just below the cover.

After all, Truth is like a Woman's breast.

Perfect. Until the time it's Half Covered.

The Lonely Flower & Smiling Petals

Everybody thinks the Flower is a success!

Perfectly Bloomed, in its best form of Fragrance, totally in awe by everybody who sees it.

Kinda living the 'anybody would want to be this' phase.

Isn't it?

But, do you know - what the Flower thinks?

I'M TRAPPED!!!

PROBABLY I'M A GOLDEN CAGE. GIVEN THE LOVE I DESERVE, BUT NOT THE ONE I NEED.

GIVEN THE NOURISHMENT I NEED BUT NOT THE FREEDOM TO ENJOY IT

Leaving me to spend every minute of the passing life in an already-created way.

And do you know what I think?

I'm just your adornment. The one you'll allow to bloom, just to cut next and add it in between your fingers of 'familyness' to take a pic and watch me crumble.

And at the end of the day, when I finally withered away, all I got was a list of regrets as to why,

"I HAVEN'T FLOWN AWAY FROM YOU SOONER WHILE I STILL HAD THE ESSENCE IN ME TO LOVE"

It was at this point that I asked myself. "Is it really life?"

And the answer I got was two faced.

"You are just kidding yourself that being between screens is life & that things will change by itself while you remain virtually a puppet living a life you regret."

And

"It's just a matter of time - hold your patience."

& That's exactly where I stand.

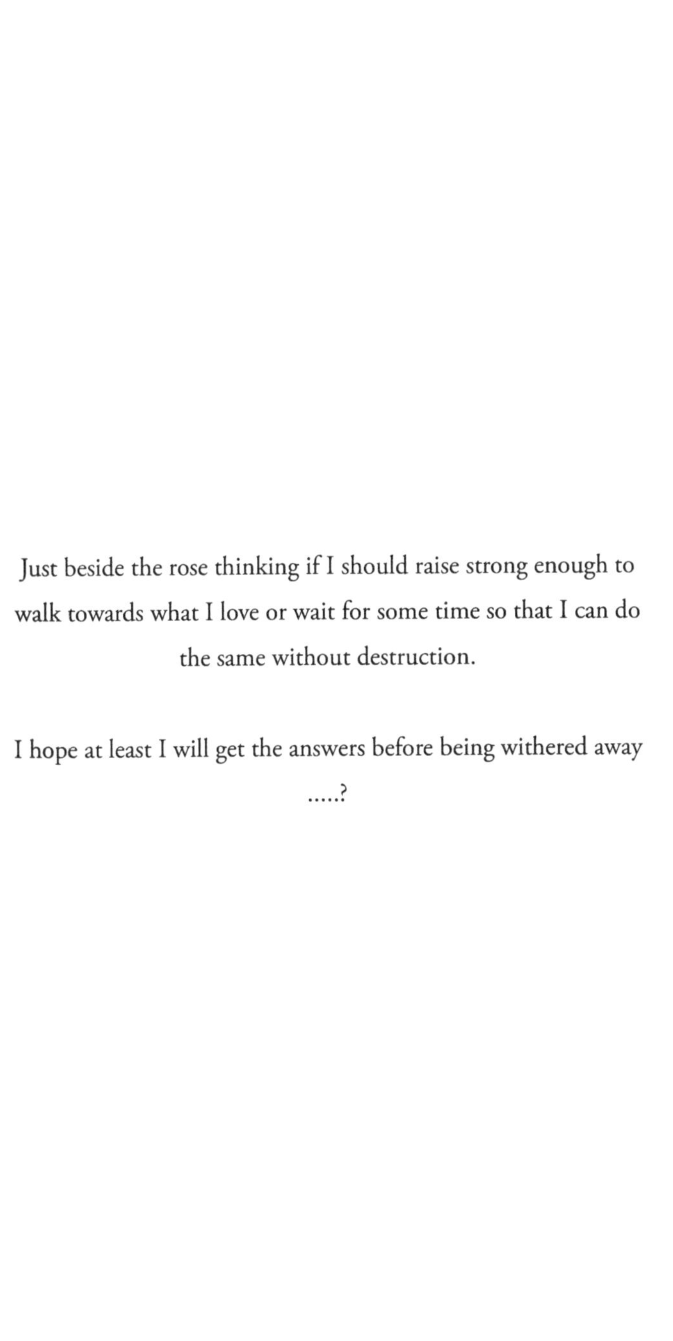

Just beside the rose thinking if I should raise strong enough to walk towards what I love or wait for some time so that I can do the same without destruction.

I hope at least I will get the answers before being withered away .....?

The Chip on your Shoulder

It's not cool. It's not casual.

But it's not deep enough.

Yes. That's the whole problem.

You won't get it when something is sooo deep, deep enough not to get out of you. But still not deep enough to not give a second thought.

Why would it happen? Why would t leave a mark? Why would it still bother you?

When you wear a chip on your shoulder - it's tough to think. It's tough to first realize there's a chip and even if you do, it's almost unrealistic to understand what kind of chip it is.

So why does it bother you? Or, what bothers you? How does it bother you? Why do you react the way you just did?

You have no answer? Yeah, probably not. Because all you knew was a volcano erupted.

What Volcano? What was it filled with? Why did it erupt? How did it erupt so suddenly?

No idea!

Why? Is it because you didn't bother to ask?

No! But because you weren't wise enough to reason.

You just responded without realizing or acknowledging if that's a worth while response.

You didn't even stand by to ask yourself if the other person deserved it.

Why?

Because you don't have the answer!

Oh is it?

Nooooo. Probably you knew the answer but were just too afraid to face it.

Spit it out!

Why?

Why?

WHYYY??????

.

.

.

.

.

I have a chip on my shoulder, a heavy load over my head, and a big bag of pride underneath - just with no Idea of How/When to unload

Or even worse,

Should It be unloaded?

That's what creates the pinnacle.

So why bother unloading it?

.

.

.

.

.

Don't say it again

In reality - the Fairytale is built over a Graveyard & Almost every Graveyard can Bloom.

You don't know when it'll be a blossom and when it'll be a insectivorous.

So if you wish for one, make sure if you can handle it.

And ask yourself - Is it Worth it!

If you ask me, it's sure as hell worth it!

But trust me, no one alongside me would say the same.

Cuz at the end of the day - they wouldn't wanna be with someone with a Chip in their shoulders!

A Page - in the Diary of my Teddy

I'm Beautiful,

I'm desirable,

I'm at my best form.

And yet, why am I alone?

Why am I left back?

Why are people laughing but never including me in it?

Why am I the only person who's being hugged only when they need?

Why are my calls of love never answered?

Why am I at a corner?

At first when they saw me, they were overjoyed. But when I became theirs - I was thrown at a corner. Useless, Never hugged, never loved. Unless they are bored.

Why?

Am I wrong?

Am I not good enough?

Am I not cute enough?

Am I not fluffy enough?

Why?... Why...?

All I wanted was to make you laugh and be with you.

But All I got was seeing you laugh forgetting me.

What should I change? How should I be?

Will I ever get you back? The same way you saw me the first time when you saw me at the store...?

At least once more, in my lifetime....

.

.

.

.

.

Never Let your Teddy/Pet feel this. Anytime.

If you can't give attention - never include it in your life.

Sun Shine or Sun Scream?

O' my dear Sun,
Do you feel trapped?
Imprisoned by your Own?
Always Protected & Secluded?
Staying Still, without movement...
While all Planets Revolve,
Nowhere to go, Nothing to do
Seeing everyone else Revolve & Rotate.

O' dear Sun,
How do you feel?
Why do you burn so much?
Is it rage? Is it Burning Desire?
Is it Anger? Is it Disappointment?
To Break the orbits & set yourself free
To Show yourself up Unpolished
Un Influenced – Just the way you wanted to be

O'my Holy Grail
May the Sun Calm Down
Let the power center subside
May the rage be tamed
For, if they break out

We would all be frozen

As the Sun takes a solo trip

Through the unspoken lands

The Night Sky

It's a Starry Night.

Not the one you would run to lie down. But the one you'll run away from.

Not the one that showers twinkling stars, but the one that throws hailstorms

Despite the Million reasons to soak up - The human soul wants to rise up & fight.

It's the lack of, idk what - that made the whirlpool spin faster.

But what made the human soul retain consistency of the never ending love still remains to be the one gaze at the third floor staircase of the old school?

In Love & Always in Love.

Let the stars shine, hailstorms come, and whirlpool spin. The holding hands wouldn't collapse at the force of the world's Anti-gravity.

#letmetellyousomething

Irrelevant? Well, who cares?

And probably, I don't give a damn!
Damnnn! Do you? Oh yeah. You should.

The Stone Paths

We all Fall,
We all Love.

We all Expect,
We all Accept

We all Lie,
We believe we can Fly.

We all cry,
Try not to die.

We all Miss,
The one person we want to Kiss.

We all Think,
Life looks better in Pink.

We all drive,
Make life Thrive.

We all sketch,
Forgetting we can Etch.

We Indulge in Fear,
Thinking of the Rear.

Forgetting we are here - Amidst the lost love & searching soul.

Thinking of a place we can hold on to - Stay anchored to.

For the rest of the life,

Which,

We all think it is long,
Forgetting we aren't Young.

To my lost drug, to my Lost Love

Pasting the hearts, Casting the cards

Thanking of you dreaming of me

Along the Path of the Forgotten Road.

Coffe in a Tea Cup

Not every tea cup holds tea.

Not every human is made for achievement.

Not every plant is made for flowering.

Not everyday the sun is meant to shine.

The bottom line is, when as humans are able to accept all of these, why are we not able to trust our own differences and accept ourselves as we are?

You don't need to be a billionaire to be satisfied with money.

You don't need to be an international chef to be able to cook good.

You don't need to be an entrepreneur to be successful.

You don't need to be a supermodel to look beautiful.

At the end of the day all you need to be is YOU.

THE SPECIAL YOU IN YOUR OWN WAY.

The Beauty of the cactus lies in its thorns.

The beauty of the sea lies in it saltiness.

The beauty of you lie in your in imperfections.

Let's be perfectly imperfect!

BUT NEVER STOP STRIVING TO BE PERFECT.

Who knows?! At the end of the day, you might even become a Billionaire, An Entrepreneur, a Chef or a Super Model!

Let's never Stop Dreaming and always stay Flying.

Afterall, Harvey Spector taught us, "Life is 'this', I Like 'THISSS' "

And I'm sure we all wanna be "THISSS."

So let's not settle for "this"

Art without a Title

This one doesn't have a Title.

.

.

This phase of life is something I can't define.

I do not know if I am happy or anguish. I do not know if I'm Safe or Trapped.

Do not know if it's the end or the start.

Do not know if life is beginning to hatch or the dream is getting shut down.

While in a corner I think of the shut down period before sunrise, the other side of the mind speaks of breakdown.

While I relish the time with family, it's a despair to not feel the outside world.

A decade from now, if I think back - when I turn 33, I do not know if I'll miss these days, or will I thank the universe from granting me the life I've dreamt of. The one that's the opposite of what's there right now.

.

.

.

It's tiredness. The lasting tiredness. To be the Sun but stay hidden. To want to Jump, but saying you are afraid of heights. To explore and yet having your limbs amputated.

To Start Flying, but forcefully put down to sleep in the basement.

They said, sometimes Love can be suffocating.

& guess what?

What's suffocating is - Giving someone your version of "Ethics" and saying "This is the only one that should be followed".

Dear,

Soon I'll Fly high. Soon, I'll get a chance to walk away from that closed gates. And trust me, the day you see me step out - you'll see me the way I am.

The way you never wanted me to be.

The way I always wanted to be.

And that day, I'll never come back..

For, the place now reminds me of agony filled cries of freedom
that I once had. Deep inside me.

And that day, you'll see who I really was.

The one beneath the social skin you draped me in.

Rehabilitation that didn't exist

"To Hold You"

was my primary notion.

LOA succeeded on a minority basis, while the heartful attraction failed predominantly.

Destiny overpowered while decoding the shittiest piece of art. - The one that the heart took a decade to carve out.

You were a drug - I once said. The society asks me now, "When are you going to your rehabilitation center?"

I ask them, "Oh, does it exist?"

Cancer in the body is fatal, they said. None remarked on the one that eats the soul alive while it screams out aloud.

Mind is a Bastard. Heart is sinister. Damn! Who tf made the soul so loyal, for it rinses out the charisma of the pleasant environment while still lurking around the one-armed fellowmen who were to die tomorrow?

Hey! Are you an oxyMORON? IDK if I love you or if I am owned by you!

Being an Entrepreneur isn't a fair deal if your heart is an employee of the old scene from the movie that flopped in the 70s.

Ufff! I hope Sidney Sheldon is alive now! The murder plots and death curves would trample at the sight of the illusion the mind creates.

Stories are a part of life. Stories are a secret wife. Stories are your agony, stories are your medicine.

But

Aren't stories bound to have a happy ending?

Childhood was a scam! I always heard, Cinderella found her prince. But never realised her step sister became psychotic because she lost her Prince...

24 Hours - I asked.

Lifetime was Gifted.

Just a difference - I asked for Reality while it was Gifted for Illusion.

The Queen of Spade

A Queen can be both!

"The Director of a corporate company walks in with elegance. The loud footsteps speak of her dashing authority.

While a lot of employees & fellow corporates raise to greet her with respect, the woman walks in with her head raised higher.

The red carpet rolls out. The BGM plays out aloud, "I'm unstoppable, I'm a Porsche with no breaks. I'm so powerful...." as she holds the mic to speak..."

On the other side of the day

"With a man of her dreams, on the drizzling beach side - collecting shells and catching crabs on a beach bucket, she laughs and rolls in sand.

Cherishing the sunset, playing with Nemo & taking off the summer bikini exposing her underboob tatoo. It was a private pool. Decorated with roses & lemon grass candles. A warm rinse of waves & a glass of champagne.

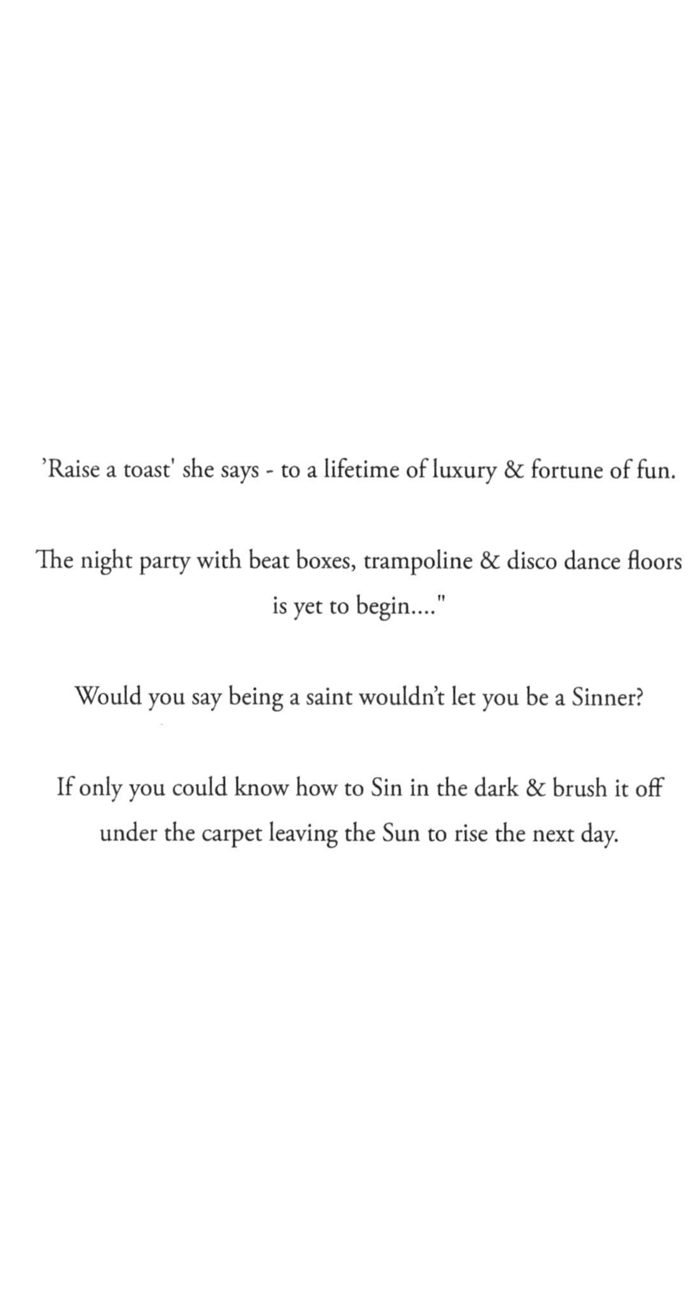

'Raise a toast' she says - to a lifetime of luxury & fortune of fun.

The night party with beat boxes, trampoline & disco dance floors is yet to begin...."

Would you say being a saint wouldn't let you be a Sinner?

If only you could know how to Sin in the dark & brush it off under the carpet leaving the Sun to rise the next day.

Passion

A couple kissing each other...

Two Parrots cherishing their "happy together" moments...

A perfect spider web adorned by crystalline water droplets...

The Soothing leaves... A Perfect sync of Passionate ideals.

Oh Really??

Is this really Passion?

Well, what if I say you Otherwise? The Real Passion here is not to rejoice but to REVOLT.

PASSION...

A ferocious Cheetah awaiting its perfect moment to attack,

A Spider web deserted by its insider leaving it to trap any other habitant getting in,

Two parrots keeping their eyes on their backs craving to hunt,

The fond memories of a lover boy who now sees his girl kissing another guy giving him a stronger reason to freeze the merry green Christmas tree into a frozen apocalypse.

The vengeance of the past awaiting to haunt the fond memories of future...

PASSION HERE LIES IN REVENGE. PASSION TO KILL,

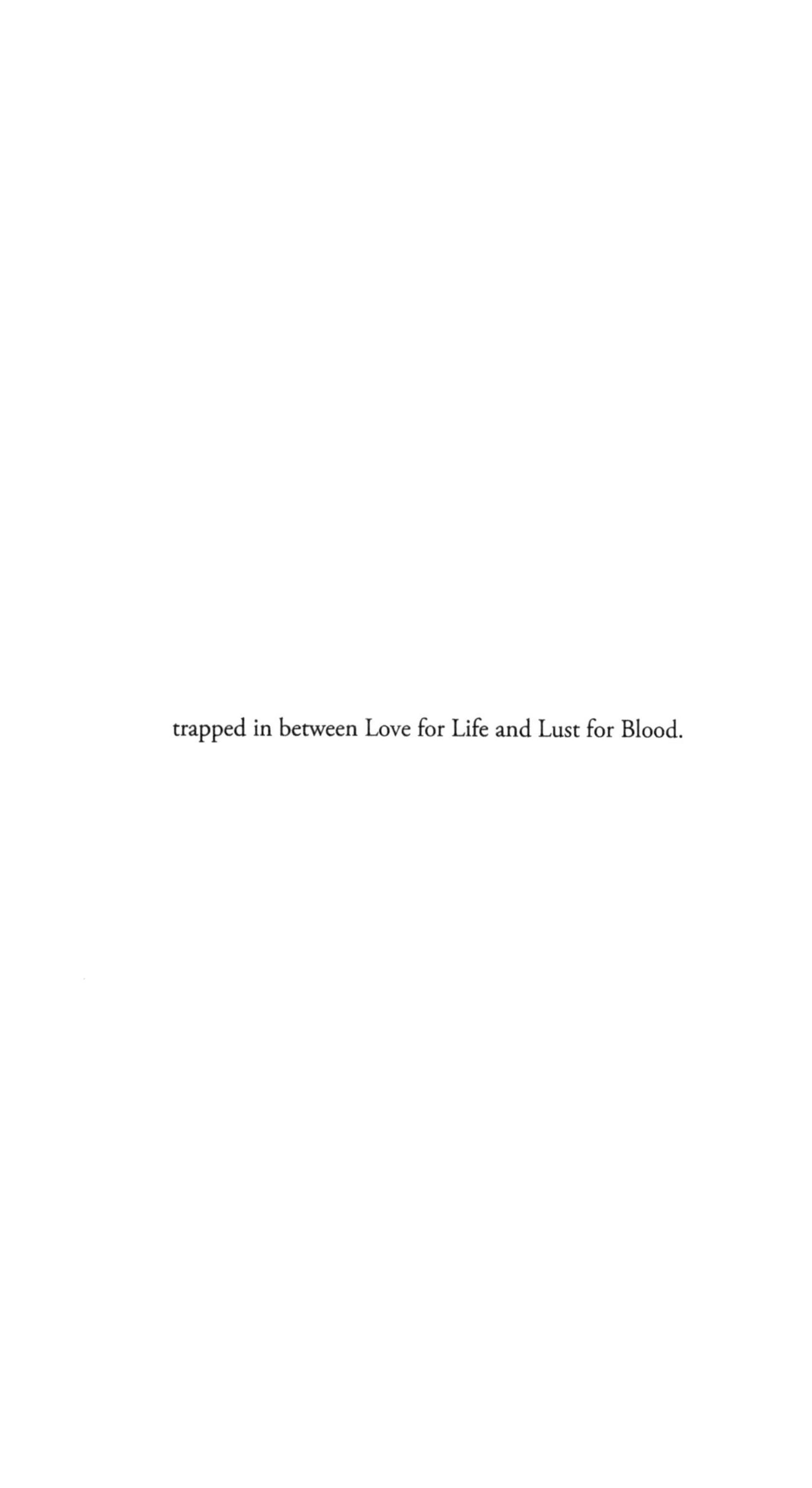

trapped in between Love for Life and Lust for Blood.

Scarlet

Enchanting beauty wrapped around in a dazzling skin.

The true embodiment of the sacred purity.

It's said that the most troubled are often the saints. May be its true when looking into the heart of scarlet.

Caught in between two acceptable shades, misery of being not recognized filled up the void causing chaos. The pretty pink flamingo getting prettier yet, looking for nectar rather than fishes.

The autumn leaves still holding on rather than falling down.

How often could this correlation between veins and lungs be seen?

Empty veins and dried up lungs.

They all tell the same story, the story of the tongue craving Lollipop, the story of the girl seeking her long gone lover boy. All supporting the story of the not recognized scarlet.

The story of the color that is stuck between the brightness of Red and Orange. The story of the perfect blend that forever creates gleam.

Scarlet- Isn't the girl...It's the color of her eyes.

The Red Sparkling Star

Staying at the epicenter of the Galaxy,
Envies the blue star without knowing it is the centrepiece

Mistaking its brightness as glare,

It gets jealous of the blue Mattestar.

Spends its life in distress, not knowing life isn't forever.

The day has come . soon gets its life out. loses its brightness and
becomes the matte Blue Star and falls down dead as a rock.

The moon Smiles with Glee.
For it has known the story as the story of every star.

It rustles itself up, and covers itself in its hidden phase with dust
twice as thick as a foil.

It has known the story of phases.

The End Note

When I die, I do not want to be burnt down to ashes.

Getting lost in less than 5 minutes .

I wanna be buried, In a velvet coffin and taking millions of minutes to fade away, and even then leaving traces behind.

Like, how can someone with so such life and dreams to be done in 5 minutes?

Huh?

Look Forward

This is the first. But this is most certainly not the Last.

Ever wondered why the Last Page of the book can still be the first page of your life's ignition?

If you choose to write rather than read.

My life started making sense every time I started writing, What I felt, what I saw, What I thought and - not to mention, What I dreamt of.

So that's how, everytime, every night in my dreams - I saw them, I felt them, and that's exactly I knew them. The Analogies, the worth of every minute and the realisation that - this Moment, this speech you just read, This is Life.

Yes! This is Life.

9 798889 599272

Printed by Libri Plureos GmbH in Hamburg, Germany